My Science Library

Reproduction in Plants

by Julie K. Lundgren

Science Content Editor:
Shirley Duke

Rourke
Educational Media

rourkeeducationalmedia.com

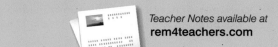
Teacher Notes available at
rem4teachers.com

Science Content Editor: Shirley Duke holds a bachelor's degree in biology and a master's degree in education from Austin College in Sherman, Texas. She taught science in Texas at all levels for twenty-five years before starting to write for children. Her science books include *You Can't Wear These Genes, Infections, Infestations, and Diseases, Enterprise STEM, Forces and Motion at Work, Environmental Disasters,* and *Gases.* She continues writing science books and also works as a science content editor.

www.rourkeeducationalmedia.com

Photo credits: Cover © Brian A Jackson, Ilyashenko Olesky; Table of Contents © leonid_tit; Page 4/5 © Bogdan Wankowicz, Jakez; Page 5 © AndreiC; Page 6 © David Monniaux, Brian A Jackson, XIIIfromTOKYO; Page 7 © François MEY, AridOcean; Page 8/9 © Andrea Danti; Page 9 © ducu59us;
Page 10/11 © SweetCrisis; Page 12 © ducu59us, Christian Lopetz; Page 13 © Gorilla; Page 14/15 © leonid_tit; Page 15 © Fotokon, Ron Rowan Photography; Page 16 © AleXoiD; Page 16/17 © Ian Lee; Page 18 © dabjola, Marjanneke de Jong; Page 19 © JIANG HONGYAN; Page 20/21 © Igor Borodin; Page 21 © Dr U, de2marco;

Editor: Kelli Hicks

My Science Library series produced by Blue Door Publishing, Florida for Rourke Educational Media.

Library of Congress PCN Data

Lundgren, Julie K.
 Reproduction in Plants / Julie K. Lundgren.
  p. cm. -- (My Science Library)
 ISBN 978-1-61810-090-0 (Hard cover) (alk. paper)
 ISBN 978-1-61810-223-2 (Soft cover)
 Library of Congress Control Number: 2012930293

Printed in China, FOFO I - Production Company
 Shenzhen, Guangdong Province

rourkeeducationalmedia.com

customerservice@rourkeeducationalmedia.com
PO Box 643328 Vero Beach, Florida 32964

Table of Contents

Plant Life Cycle

In a life cycle, plants sprout, **reproduce**, and die. Every plant must have some way to make more of its kind as part of its life cycle.

Annuals, like tomatoes, complete their life cycles in a single year. Apple trees, ferns, and other **perennials** live at least three years and may reproduce many times. Biennials, like garlic plants, take two years to complete their life cycles.

Many garden sunflowers sprout, flower, make seeds, and die in one growing season. Other varieties are perennials.

Plant species use different ways to reproduce. Millions of years ago early plants reproduced by making spores. Ferns still use this method today. More modern plants make seeds and flowers. Others reproduce by cloning. These plants grow new plants from the stems, roots, or leaves of a single parent plant.

Ferns reproduce with spores.

Dandelions reproduce with seeds.

Bamboo reproduces by cloning.

More than 300,000 plants live on Earth. More await discovery in remote areas, such as the Amazon rainforest in South America and the wild river valleys of Southeast Asia.

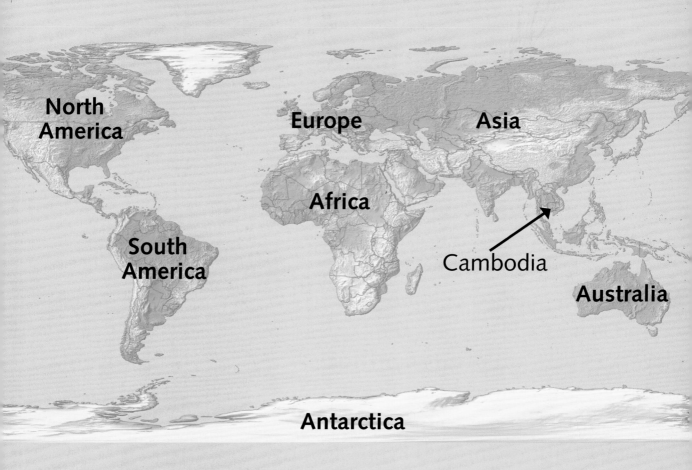

North America

Europe

Asia

Africa

Cambodia

South America

Australia

Antarctica

In Cambodia, scientists recently found several new plant species, including a strange, red pitcher plant that traps insects in its center.

Parts of a Plant

Special parts allow plants to fill their needs for sunlight, water, and **nutrients**. Each part has a function. Roots take up nutrients and water from the soil. Stems provide a pipeline between the roots and leaves and support the leaves. Leaves perform **photosynthesis**. They capture light energy from the Sun and use it to make simple sugars for growing and living. During photosynthesis, leaves take in carbon dioxide and give off oxygen.

light energy

carbon dioxide

Photosynthesis

roots

water

Flowers and Seeds

Flowering plants make seeds. Just as plants have special parts for photosynthesis, flowers have parts with special jobs for seed making. Inside the flower's petals are female parts called pistils. Pistils have three parts: the stigma, the style, and the ovary. Inside the ovary, seeds form. Male flower parts include filaments, each topped by a sticky anther. Anthers make **pollen**. The filaments and anthers make the stamen.

Parts of a Flower

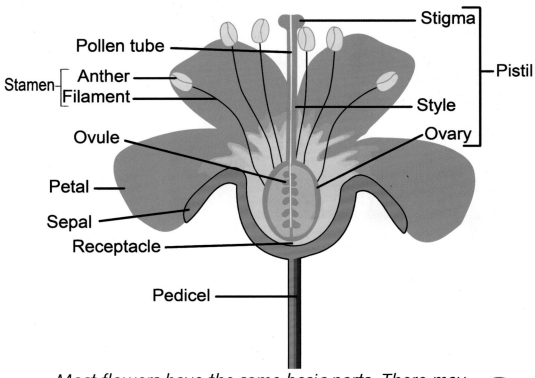

Stigma

Pollen tube

Stamen— Anther
Filament

Pistil

Style

Ovule

Ovary

Petal

Sepal

Receptacle

Pedicel

Most flowers have the same basic parts. There may be some variation depending on the plant species.

oxygen

To make seeds, flowers must receive pollen on their own pistil or from another plant of their kind. Pollen can travel on the wind or be carried by nectar-drinking animals called pollinators. Colorful, scented petals serve as flags to passing pollinators, waving them in for a taste of nectar and a dusting of pollen.

Night Bloomers

Saguaro cactus

Some flowers bloom only at night. To attract pollinators in the dark, they rely on pale petals and strong scents. The scent in flowers comes from oils in their petals.

As bats, birds, and insects feed, pollen sticks to their bodies. It brushes off on the next flower, helping the process of pollination.

To make seeds, pollen must land on the stigma. A tiny tube then grows from the pollen grain down inside the style to the ovules inside the ovary.

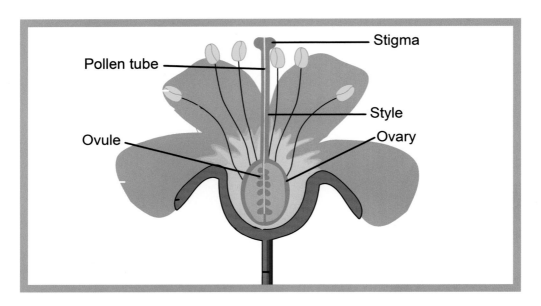

As seeds form in the ovules, the ovary gets bigger.

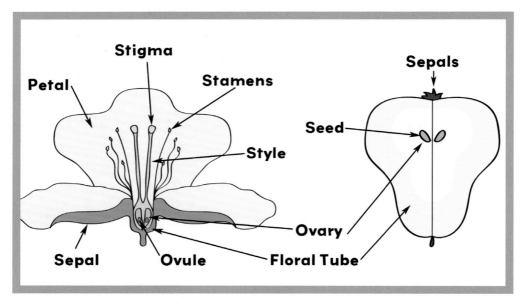

In some plants, the ovary becomes a fruit and the ovules become seeds.

Once the seeds germinate, the seed coat cracks open and the tiny plant appears. The stem and leaves grow toward the Sun and the roots grow downward.

Many seeds have a shell, seed coat, and kernel. The kernel holds the beginnings of a new plant's roots, stem, and leaves, plus a bit of stored food to help the plant begin to grow. Seeds **germinate** only in the right conditions. Soil temperature, the amount of daylight or darkness, oxygen levels, and water availability all play a role in germination for various seeds. In some ecosystems, like prairies and lodgepole pine forests, fires trigger seed germination.

Might As Well Be Walking

Seeds have developed adaptations for getting around so they can start growing in new places. Dandelion and maple tree seeds can drift and spin in the wind, while some squirrels collect and bury tasty acorns. Other seeds burst from exploding seedpods like little fireworks, and still others hitchhike on a passing animal's fur coat, like the hooked seedpods of burr clover and the devil's claw. Adaptations such as these help plant species survive.

dandelion

Each dandelion seed is attached to a little white parachute structure. When the seeds ripen, just a puff of wind sends them sailing away.

Dandelion Life Cycle

When a dandelion seed lands in moist soil, it sprouts. It grows a single, long, fat root called a taproot. It grows green leaves and, after several weeks, flower buds. When insects pollinate the bright yellow flowers, new seeds develop.

tap root →

Squirrels bury nuts and seeds for later use, but do not use all they bury. Those left behind or forgotten sprout.

Orange jewelweed makes seedpods that explode when ripe.

15

Spores, Clones, and Cones

Flowerless plants reproduce in other ways. Mosses and ferns make spores. Spores have only one cell and do not have food storage like seeds do. These cells give rise to new plants without using pollen or flowers. Conifers produce seeds inside cones instead of flowers. Cones need pollen to make seeds. In flowerless plants, only wind carries pollen and spores, not insects.

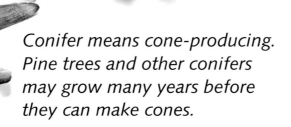

Conifer means cone-producing. Pine trees and other conifers may grow many years before they can make cones.

Spores on the underside of fern leaves produce and release spores.

Grasses, tulips, and potatoes may produce seeds, but more commonly reproduce by sprouting from underground stems. The offspring of these plants are **clones** of the parent plant. The underground, reproductive stems take different forms depending on the plant. In grasses, these stems, called **rhizomes**, grow out from the parent plant and sprout new plants along the way.

daffodils

rhizome

If plants have rhizomes you can snip between the sprouts to divide the plants.

bulb

Onions, tulips, and daffodils grow from bulbs.

Tulips grow from bulbs, another kind of underground stem. Bulbs have future leaves, stems, and flowers covered in special food storage leaves and a papery wrapper. **Tubers**, such as potatoes, do not have leaves for food storage, but instead store food inside the stem itself. When we eat potatoes, we are eating the fattened, reproductive stem.

Potatoes sprout from small dimples called eyes.

Strawberry plants make clones, too. They have special, above ground stems called runners that grow out from the parent plant. A runner can put down roots and sprout a new plant. Some kinds of strawberries and grasses can grow from seeds, too.

Look at the plants around you and discover how they reproduce. Watch that life cycle!

runner

Clones of Your Own

Grow some clones using organic potatoes. Put potatoes in a paper bag with a whole apple. Fold the top of the bag down and let it sit for a week to sprout the potatoes. When they have sprouted, handle gently. Cut the potatoes into chunks, each having two to three sprouts. Plant them about 2 inches (5 centimeters) deep in large pots or in a sunny garden space and water regularly. The new plants should come up within two weeks.

Show What You Know

1. What are some ways pollen can travel from one flower to another?

2. How are bulbs different than tubers?

3. How can a plant's adaptations for reproduction help it survive? Give an example.

Glossary

annuals (AN-yoo-uhlz): plants that grow only one season and must start from seed each year

clones (KLOHNZ): offspring identical to their single parent plant

germinate (JUR-muh-nate): send out a root and shoot from a seed

nutrients (NOO-tree-uhnts): vitamins and minerals in the soil that are needed by plants to stay healthy and grow

perennials (puh-REN-ee-uhlz): plants that sprout again each year without replanting

photosynthesis (foh-toh-SIN-thuh-siss): the process by which green plants transform the Sun's energy into food using carbon dioxide and water and produce oxygen

pollen (POL-uhn): the golden dust that flowers make for seed production

reproduce (ree-pruh-DOOSS): make more of something

rhizomes (RYE-zohmz): underground stems that grow out from the parent plant and sprout new plants exactly like the parent plant, commonly found in grasses

tubers (TOO-burz): large, underground stems that some plants, like potatoes, use for food storage and reproduction

Index

Websites to Visit

www.ecokids.ca/pub/kids_home.cfm

http://urbanext.illinois.edu/gpe/case4/index.html

www.biology4kids.com/files/plants_reproduction.html

About the Author

Julie K. Lundgren has written more than 40 nonfiction books for children. She gets a kick out of sharing juicy facts about science, nature, and animals, especially if they are slightly disgusting! Through her work, she hopes kids will learn that Earth is an amazing place and young people can make a big difference in keeping our planet healthy. She lives in Minnesota with her family.

Ask The Author!
www.rem4students.com